Fire!

Written by Sue Gunningham

Contents	Page
Chapter 1. *Wildfire Alert!*	4
Chapter 2. *Out Of Control*	10
Chapter 3. *Hazardous Work*	14
Chapter 4. *No Time For Games*	18
Chapter 5. *Trapped!*	22
Chapter 6. *Mission Accomplished*	26
Photo Feature: *Wildfires And The Environment*	30
Index And Bookweb Links	32
Glossary	Inside Back Cover

Rigby

Fire!

This exciting story takes place in Australia. Although the fire reported in this story takes place 10,000 miles away from the United States, it is like the frequent wildfires we read about in places closer to home . . .

Wildfires have raged across parts of California, Alaska, and other U.S. states.

Chapter Snapshots ...

1. Wildfire Alert!
Everyone's on full alert at Fire Headquarters. Crew 24 must be ready for action!

2. Out Of Control
A fire is raging out of control and is threatening to burn down people's homes!

3. Hazardous Work
Everyone is working hard to prevent the fire from reaching the houses.

4. No Time For Games
A little dog follows the crew as they try to control the raging fire.

5. Trapped!
On a forest road, a family is in great danger!

6. Mission Accomplished
The crew is tired and needs to rest; after a day of danger, there is a happy reunion.

1. Wildfire Alert!

Chief Fire Officer Cooper stared at the huge, electronic weather map on the wall at Fire Headquarters. The weather stations were reporting hot, northerly winds gusting over 30 miles per hour, with no rainfall likely for 48 hours. Satellite photographs showed a high level of dryness in the grasslands and forests across the state.

After checking the locations of small fires already reported, he reached for the telephone.

"Chief Fire Officer Cooper here," he stated. "I'm declaring tomorrow a day of Total Fire Ban. No one will be able to light a fire outdoors."

There are three things that fire needs to burn: fuel, heat, and oxygen.

Within minutes, volunteer firefighters all over the area were contacted by pager. They were immediately on alert for the possibility of wildfires. The evening newspapers and radio and television newscasts warned people of the following day's Total Fire Ban.

Total Fire Ban (TFB)

"Total Fire Ban" days occur in Australia on days of extreme fire risk. On these days, temperatures are very high, there is little moisture in the air, forests are dry, and strong winds are expected. Fire Headquarters tries to tell the media the night before a TFB day, so that all news broadcasts and newspapers can warn people. It is illegal to light any fires outdoors on a TFB day.

Around five o'clock that afternoon, volunteer firefighter Captain Davies received a pager message telling him that a fire had broken out near Scrubby Creek. Locking up his butcher shop, he hurried to the fire station at the end of the street.

How Do Firefighters Know There Is A Fire?

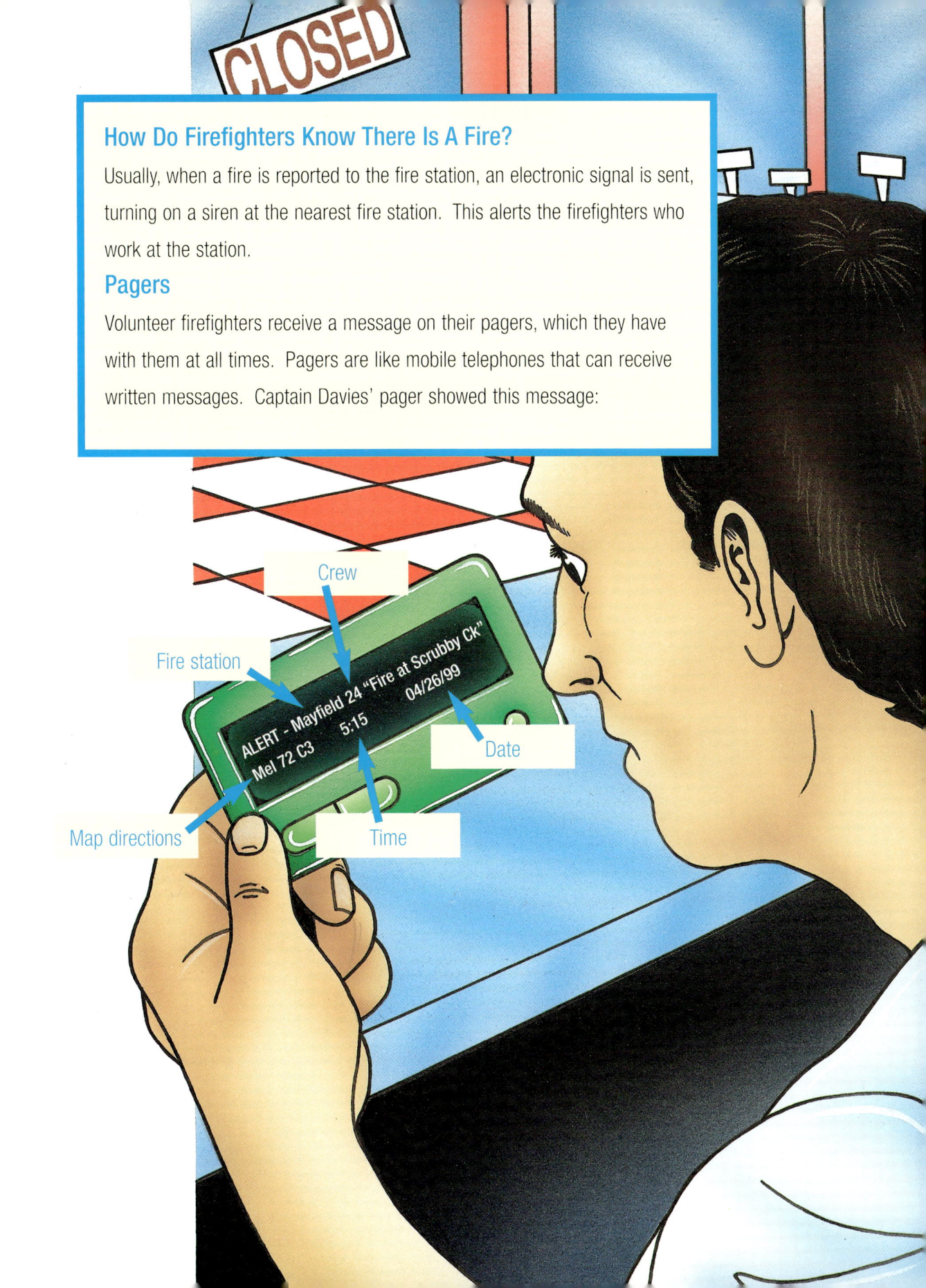

Usually, when a fire is reported to the fire station, an electronic signal is sent, turning on a siren at the nearest fire station. This alerts the firefighters who work at the station.

Pagers

Volunteer firefighters receive a message on their pagers, which they have with them at all times. Pagers are like mobile telephones that can receive written messages. Captain Davies' pager showed this message:

ALERT - Mayfield 24 "Fire at Scrubby Ck" 5:15 04/26/99
Mel 72 C3

- Crew
- Fire station
- Date
- Time
- Map directions

The other volunteers were already pulling on their special protective clothing as Captain Davies arrived. Within minutes, the fire truck pulled out of the station with sirens screaming and lights flashing.

Firefighting Equipment

Fire trucks carry many different types of equipment, including:

- **Tools to clear vegetation**—axes, spades, chain saws, rakes, hoes
- **Water equipment**—hoses, pumps, buckets
- **Protective wear**—breathing masks and air tanks
- **Special clothing**—gas and chemical splash suits
- **Rescue tools**—ropes, ladders, chains, jacks
- **Medical supplies**—first aid kit

Firefighter Rachel Williams, who was sitting next to Captain Davies, read her map and called out directions.

"Fire Headquarters, this is Crew 24 in the Mayfield truck on the way to Scrubby Creek," she radioed.

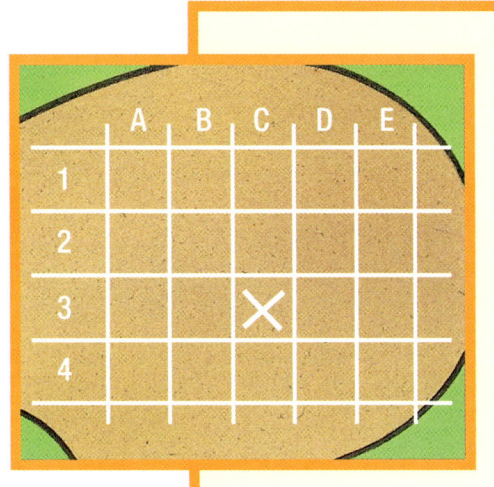

Map Reading

Firefighters read maps to find fires quickly. The maps are drawn on grids like this one. Across the top of this map there are letters on each grid line. Down the side, each grid line has a number. The map reading C3 is the place where the grid line marked "C" meets the grid line marked "3."

2. Out Of Control

The truck stopped on a dirt road beside Scrubby Creek. Two kangaroos bounded out from the smoke-filled gully and a flock of cockatoos screeched overhead.

"In the brush, over there!" shouted Captain Davies. Rachel and another volunteer, Spiro, attached the hoses to the water pump. The other firefighters rolled the hoses out and connected the nozzles to them.

A surface fire.

Types Of Wildfires

There are three main types of wildfires:
- **Ground fires** burn in roots and under the ground in peat and coal. They smolder for months with hardly any flames.
- **Surface fires** are the most common wildfires. They burn in grasses, twigs, and shrubs.
- **Crown fires** run up trunks and into the treetops. In forests, these fires spread quickly from one tree to another.

Special Protective Clothing

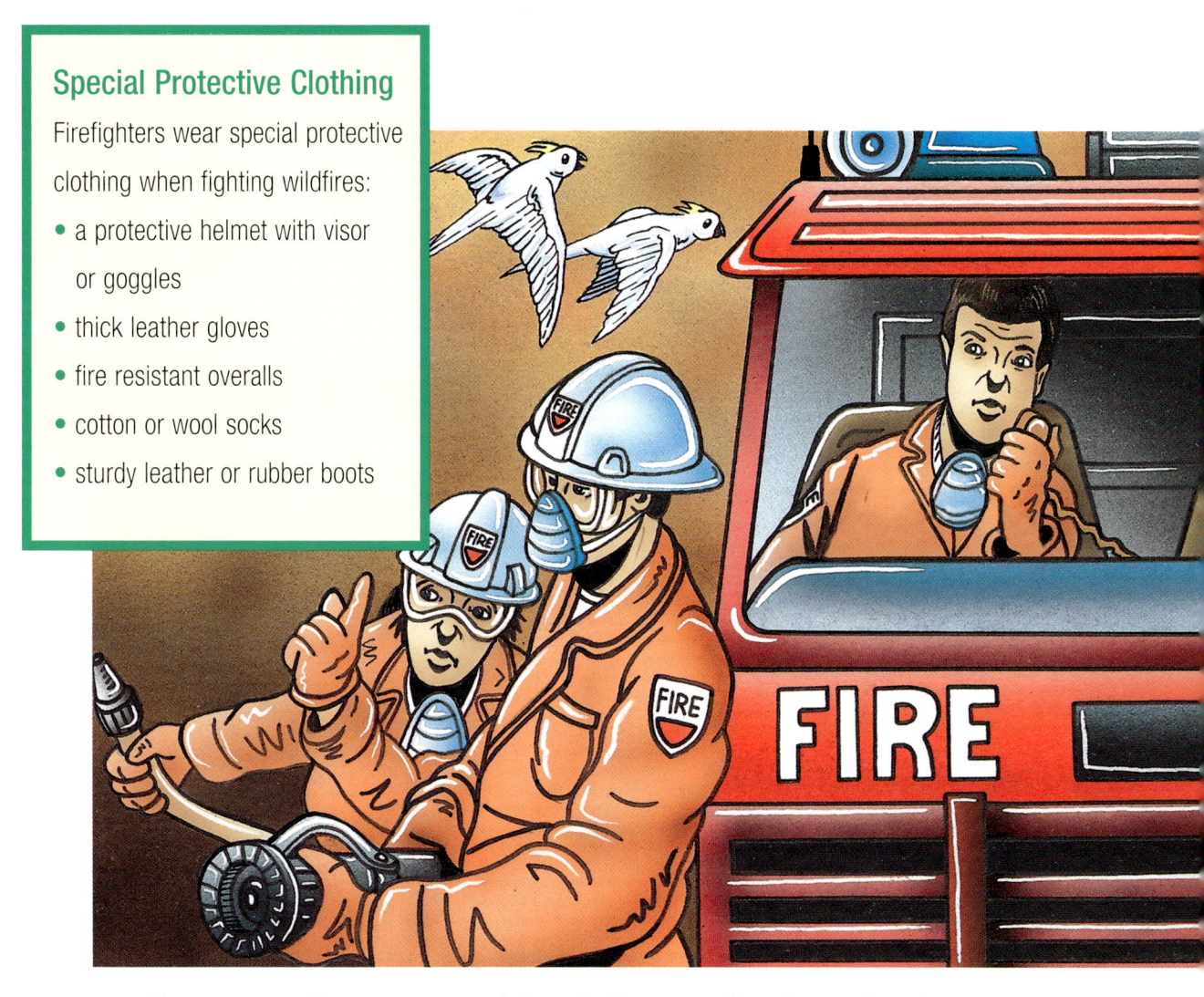

Firefighters wear special protective clothing when fighting wildfires:
- a protective helmet with visor or goggles
- thick leather gloves
- fire resistant overalls
- cotton or wool socks
- sturdy leather or rubber boots

Captain Davies grabbed the radio handset.

"The fire's burning in undergrowth in the valley. With this wind, it might change to a crown fire in the forest nearby and threaten the houses on top of the hill! We need at least one more truck over on the east side of the valley to help us out!"

The firefighters could feel the hot ashes on their faces. As the smoke cloud became worse, they put on their goggles to protect their eyes. The taste of soot was strong in their throats.

Experience told them that this might be a long battle, so they tried to relax and settle into a routine to be sure they'd last the day.

It was not long before Crew 24 heard the arrival of the support team's trucks across the valley to the east. Headquarters radioed Captain Davies to explain that police were now stopping traffic from entering the area.

Suddenly, a blast of hot air rushed up behind the firefighters, pushing the fire to the top of the trees ahead.

Warning Signs Of Wildfire

People should be on the alert when traveling in dry, grassy areas during summer. Early signs of possible wildfire activity include:

- hot weather and strong southerly winds
- distressed animals
- no bird sounds
- haze or smoke columns
- burned leaves or ash blowing in the wind
- a smell of smoke

"It's too dangerous! We can't control it from down here!" yelled Captain Davies. "Everyone, back in the truck!"

3. Hazardous Work

Crew 24 drove back onto the main road to move higher up the hill above the fire. Gusty winds were blowing hot ash ahead of the flames, and the crew could see many spot fires starting all over the forest.

"I hope the town's people have decided to evacuate their homes!" shouted firefighter Max Evans, who was sitting alongside Captain Davies in the truck.

The crew could hear the roar of the wildfire as it grew in size and speed and rushed up the hillside.

Spot Fires

Spot fires begin from sparks and ash being blown on the wind ahead of a fire. In Australia, gum trees are a real danger in wildfires because their eucalyptus oil helps wildfires to keep burning, and their stringy bark is easily blown by the wind.

Why Does Australia Have So Many Wildfires?

Australia is among the world's most fire-prone countries. The winter rainfall and dry spring weather in the southern and eastern areas of Australia are very good for plant growth. The hot summers dry out this plant growth, making it dangerous fuel for wildfires, or bushfires, as they are called there.

Key

- Lots of forest fuel
- Lots of grass fuel
- Some grass fuel
- Not much fuel at all

Fire Burns Faster Uphill

Flames always burn upward. That means that flames on a hill reach over the new fuel, heating it up. This dries the fuel and it burns fast. The hot air from the fire rises and moves uphill, carrying the fire with it. Fires can travel at up to 12 miles per hour!

Stopping the truck, they set to work again, cutting undergrowth and hosing the forest ahead of the fire. Captain Davies radioed for more support and Fire Headquarters sent extra trucks and a pumper truck from nearby fire stations.

Special airplanes were placed on stand-by and helicopters circled above, sending information about the fire back to Headquarters.

Air Support

During times of high fire danger, the U.S. Forest Service uses helicopters and airplanes for fire spotting and fire attack. Some aircraft have "belly" water tanks that can hover over dams, pumping up to 2,340 gallons of water into their tanks in 38 seconds.

> **Fire-breaks**
>
> Firefighters may try to make a fire-break by destroying vegetation ahead of the main fire front. Bulldozers are often used to do this. Sometimes, this "fuel" is destroyed by lighting small fires ahead of the main fire. These small fires burn back, toward the main fire. This is called "back burning."

Captain Davies' crew was soon joined by many other firefighters. Some teams worked on both sides of the fire, trying to put out the flames, while others worked to clear a fire-break ahead of the fire front.

Captain Davies and Max were hosing an area near an old, run-down house with a dry, overgrown garden. Leaves filled the spouting, and piles of wood and trash were stacked around the yard.

"It'll be hard to save that house!" yelled Max against the roar of the fire.

4. No Time For Games

Just then, a small, black dog came running from the old house, carrying a stick. He ran up to Captain Davies and dropped the stick at his feet. He wagged his tail, hoping for a game.

"Not now. Go home, boy!" said Captain Davies, rushing past him. The dog picked up the stick and ran after the firefighters.

"Water's getting low. We need a refill!" Rachel yelled to Spiro. "There's a dam two blocks away."

Spiro drove to the dam and pumped water into the tanker. The dog followed them to the dam and ran around excitedly, dropping the stick and barking.

Different Fire Trucks For Different Jobs

Tankers

Tanker trucks are used in wildfires. They can get water from dams and creeks. Some tankers are large enough to carry 780 gallons of water. Firefighters can stand on the back of a tanker to hose the fire as the tanker moves along.

Pumpers

Pumper trucks are used in towns and cities. They carry about 470 gallons of water and can pump water from city fire hydrants. Lockers on the sides of pumpers hold firefighting tools and special equipment.

"Crazy dog," said Rachel, throwing the stick as far as she could. The dog ran after it.

Driving back to the fire front, Captain Davies noticed a man dressed in shorts trying to save his house by hosing it down. He ordered Spiro to slow down as he leaned out of the window.

"Leave the area! You'll be killed by the radiant heat if the fire comes up here!" he called to the man.

The Effects Of Fire On The Body

- **Dehydration**—Your body can sweat out half a gallon of water each hour when close to a fire. You need to replace this by drinking extra water.
- **Smoke**—Breathing in smoke can hurt your throat and upset your lungs. Keep low and wear a scarf over your mouth and nose.
- **Radiant Heat**—Skin can be badly burned by the hot air ahead of a fire. Dress properly and take cover behind a wall if possible.

The man waved and got into his car. As the tanker moved off, the black dog came running up beside it. Spiro drove slowly so that the firefighters on the back could hose both sides of the road. They sometimes squirted the dog when he was in their way.

Radiant Heat

Radiant heat is the heat in the air ahead of the flames in a wildfire. It scorches plants and can burn people and animals, even before the flames reach them. Radiant heat cannot pass through solid objects. If a wildfire is close, stay inside and cover up, to protect yourself from radiant heat. Wear clothing made from wool or cotton material and choose solid shoes, socks, a long-sleeved sweater, long pants, and a strong hat. A scarf over your mouth helps to keep smoke out of your lungs.

5. Trapped!

Little did Crew 24 know that down in the forest below them, a family was trapped in their car. They had been on a picnic when the fire began and now the road was blocked by flames.

With everyone in the car, the father parked in the middle of the road, where there was very little fuel for the fire.

"Wind up the windows," he told his family. The mother sat in the back with the son. The daughter climbed into the front beside the father.

If You Are Trapped In A Car During A Wildfire

Check weather reports and try not to be in a forest on days when wildfire is a possibility. If you are caught, park the car in an open space, leaving the headlights on so that you can be seen in the smoke. Get down low with the windows wound up and pull a wool blanket over your body for protection from radiant heat. Never get out and run. It is highly unlikely that the gas tank will explode, but you will almost certainly die or be badly burned if you are outside as the fire passes by.

Family should have stayed in car

During wildfires in Lara, Victoria, 1969, 17 people died on a major highway. A family of five left their car and tried to outrun the fire. The entire family was killed by radiant heat a few feet from the car. Other people survived the fire by staying in their cars with the windows rolled up until the fire front had passed.

"Now, it's going to get very hot," warned the father. "I want us to get down on the floor as low as we can with these wool blankets over us. Stay down and soon the fire will pass. I know you're scared, but I also know that we can survive this."

They hugged each other and covered themselves with the blankets.

Before long, they could hear the roar of the fire. The car became very hot, and one window cracked loudly, making the little girl scream. Her father hugged her close as she began to cry.

Within minutes, the fire front had passed. The family waited until it was safe to sit up. All around them was blackened forest and smoking grass.

"We're OK," said the mother, reaching over to hug her son.

6. Mission Accomplished

Emergency Workers

There are many emergency services working to help people during wildfires. Police, firefighters, and medical workers are helped by many other organizations, such as the Red Cross and other local community groups. These organizations do many jobs, such as searching for missing people and providing food, first aid, and phone hotlines to keep family and friends informed.

Captain Davies was very tired. He looked at his watch. It was almost midnight. He radioed Fire Headquarters for a new team of firefighters to be sent to the fire front, so that Crew 24 could have a rest.

"All aboard for the Shelter," yelled Captain Davies to his team. They rolled up the hoses and climbed into the tanker.

Spiro drove to Mayfield Hall Shelter. Inside, emergency workers were writing down the names of the people who were there and giving out food, drinks, and blankets.

An emergency worker gave the firefighters drinks and sandwiches. Captain Davies looked at his crew. They were dirty and tired, but he was very proud of them. He left the group and walked outside.

Sitting on a step with a coffee mug, Captain Davies heard a soft noise nearby. The little black dog came slowly out of the darkness. Seeing Captain Davies, he wagged his tail and lay down at his feet.

Shelters

Most towns have decided on one building, such as the local hall, that will be used as an emergency shelter, where people needing food, clothing, shelter, and first aid will be looked after. People can contact the shelter to check that their family and friends are safe.

"So you made it, old boy," said Captain Davies softly, as he bent down and rubbed the dog's head. "I'll get you some water."

As Captain Davies carried a bowl of water out of the hall, his pager beeped. He read the message: "Fire under control. Crew 24 no longer needed."

Captain Davies sat watching, as the dog drank thirstily. A police car stopped outside the shelter. The family from the forest had been rescued by police passing along the road a few minutes after the fire was out.

The little girl hopped out and ran toward Captain Davies.
"Digger! Digger! You found our dog!" she called out happily.

"He ran away from our picnic when he saw the fire coming," she said to Captain Davies. The girl hugged Digger and carried him back to the family.

The wildfire was over, but the day of Total Fire Ban was just beginning. Captain Davies stood up. It was time to go home.

Wildfires And The Environment

Plants

- **Tree tops**—harmed or killed
- **Tree trunks**—outside bark burned off completely
- **Shrubs**—totally burned
- **Leaf litter**—totally destroyed
- **Soil**—some erosion after the fire

Animals

- **Insects**—many deaths among those living in leaf litter (Those that live on the tree trunks burrow inside to safety.)
- **Birds**—become confused in the smoke and many die
- **Mammals**—many die from breathing in smoke or inability to outrun the fire

But ...

Some plants need fire to free their seeds from hard, wooden seed pods. Unless there is a wildfire, new seeds and new plants will not grow.

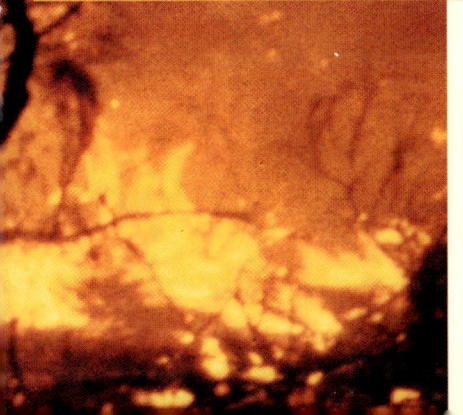

Index

aircraft 16
Australia 15
back burning 17
car safety 23
crown fire 10
dehydration 20
emergency workers 26, 27
environment 31
fire-breaks 17
firefighting equipment 8, 19
ground fire 10
map reading 9
pagers 7
protective clothing 11
pumpers 19
radiant heat 20, 21
shelter 27
smoke 20
spot fire 14
surface fire 10
tankers 8, 19
Total Fire Ban 6
U.S. Forest Service 16
warning signs 13

Fire!

More Bookweb books about emergencies!

Beyond The Black Hole—Fiction
Blackout!—Fiction
Capsize!—Fiction
Keep Calm!—Fiction

Key To Bookweb Fact Boxes
☐ Arts
☐ Health
☐ Science
☐ Social Studies
☐ Technology